Where Do Frogs Come From?

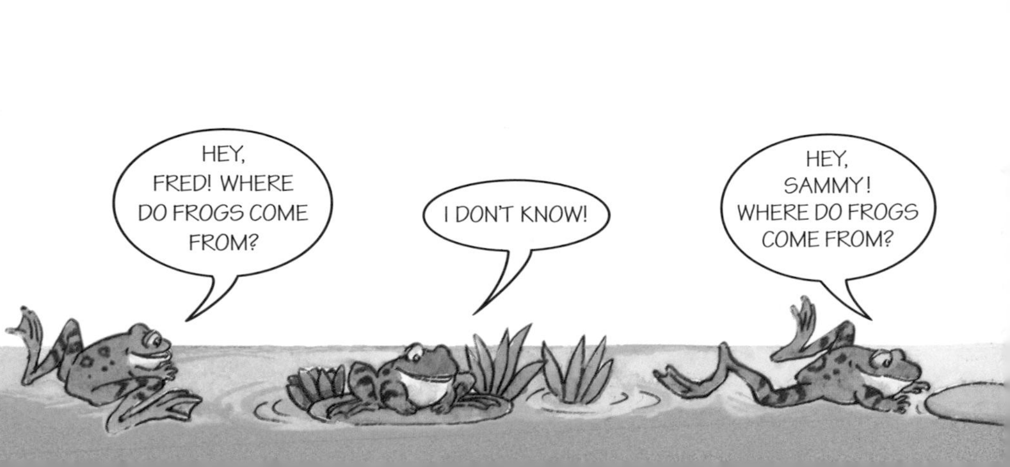

Where Do Frogs Come From?

Alex Vern

Green Light Readers
Harcourt, Inc.

Orlando   Austin   New York   San Diego   London

This big frog came from a small egg.

The black dots on this plant are frog eggs.

Pop, pop, pop!

When a frog egg hatches,
a tadpole pops out.

At first, the tadpole has a long
tail and a big body.

It looks for plants in the pond.
It eats the plants and grows very fast.

Soon the tadpole grows two
strong back legs. They help it
to kick and swim fast.

A tadpole has to swim
fast or a fish will eat it.

Small front legs form next.
The tadpole is almost a frog,
but it still has a tail.

At last the tail is gone.
The tadpole is now a
full-grown frog.

The frog is big and strong.
It can hop to find food or
run from danger.

Hop, hop!

The frog is also fast!
It eats lots of bugs.

Watch out fly!
Mmmm!

From Egg to Frog

1. Egg

2. Tadpole

3. Frog

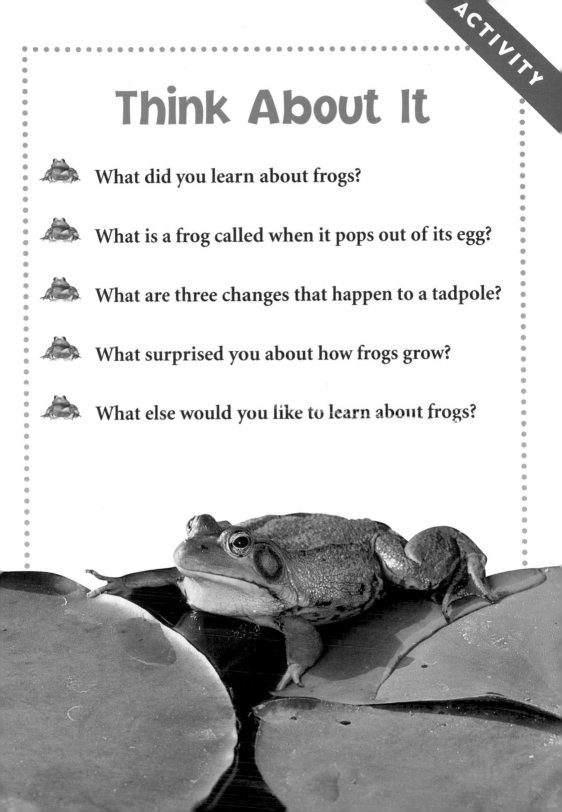

Think About It

What did you learn about frogs?

What is a frog called when it pops out of its egg?

What are three changes that happen to a tadpole?

What surprised you about how frogs grow?

What else would you like to learn about frogs?

FROG  CHAIN

Make a paper chain that shows how tadpoles become frogs.

WHAT YOU'LL NEED

- paper
- scissors
- crayons or markers
- tape

1. **Think about how tadpoles change.**

2. **Draw the five changes on paper strips.**

3. **Make the paper strips into a chain. Connect each picture with a blank paper strip.**

4. **Share your frog chain with a friend. Tell about each picture.**

Frog or Toad?

Learn how frogs are different from toads.
Make a chart.
Share what you find out with a friend!

Frogs and Toads are different.

Frogs	Toads
live in water smooth skin	live on land rough skin

A Tadpole Tale

Lots of things happen in a tadpole's life!
Make up a story about a tadpole.
It can be real or make-believe.

For information about permission to reproduce selections from this book, write to trade.permissions@hmhco.com or to Permissions, Houghton Mifflin Harcourt Publishing Company, 3 Park Avenue, 19th Floor, New York, New York 10016.

www.hmhco.com

First Green Light Readers edition 2001
Green Light Readers is a trademark of Harcourt, Inc., registered in the United States of America and/or other jurisdictions.

The Library of Congress has cataloged an earlier edition as follows:
Vern, Alex.
Where do frogs come from?/by Alex Vern.
p.   cm.
"Green Light Readers."
1. Frogs—Development—Juvenile literature.
[1. Tadpoles.   2. Frogs.]   I. Title.   II. Series.
QL668.E2V47   2001
[E]—dc21   2001001481
ISBN 978-0-15-204884-6
ISBN 978-0-15-204844-0 (pb)

RDT 19 18 17
4500650697

Ages 5–7
Grade: 1
Guided Reading Level: E–F
Reading Recovery Level: 11–12

Green Light Readers
For the reader who's ready to GO!

"A must-have for any family with a beginning reader."—*Boston Sunday Herald*

"You can't go wrong with adding several copies of these terrific books to your beginning-to-read collection."—*School Library Journal*

"A winner for the beginner."—*Booklist*

Five Tips to Help Your Child Become a Great Reader

1. Get involved. Reading aloud to and with your child is just as important as encouraging your child to read independently.

2. Be curious. Ask questions about what your child is reading.

3. Make reading fun. Allow your child to pick books on subjects that interest her or him.

4. Words are everywhere—not just in books. Practice reading signs, packages, and cereal boxes with your child.

5. Set a good example. Make sure your child sees YOU reading.

Why Green Light Readers Is the Best Series for Your New Reader

● Created exclusively for beginning readers by some of the biggest and brightest names in children's books

● Reinforces the reading skills your child is learning in school

● Encourages children to read—and finish—books by themselves

● Offers extra enrichment through fun, age-appropriate activities unique to each story

● Incorporates characteristics of the Reading Recovery program used by educators

● Developed with Harcourt School Publishers and credentialed educational consultants